Side Hustle

G

Learn How to Start a Side Business and to How to Grow That Business So That You Can Quit Your Job and the Rat Race and Start Living the Life of Your Design

By Adam Torbert

circumstances is the author responsible for any losses, direct or indirect, which are incurred as a result of the use of information contained within this document, including, but not limited to, —errors, omissions, or inaccuracies.

Contents

Thank you for buying this book and I hope that you will find it useful. If you will want to share your thoughts on this book, you can do so by leaving a review on the Amazon page, it helps me out a lot.

Chapter 1: Get In The Proper Attitude

Lots of people are so thrilled when they see a side hustle chance they believe is going to be a great fit for them. They make strategies and visualize how they're going to spend their additional money, or how they will quit their jobs the minute their side hustle blasts off.

However, prior to even getting halfway to success, they quit suddenly. They make excuses regarding why their side hustle isn't taking off. They are going to inform themselves that their day job is easier since they get a stable income on a monthly basis. They are going to attempt to persuade themselves that they're more satisfied at their day jobs nonetheless.

Lots of people have what it requires to be successful. They have the talent and the abilities to do so. However, the minute life tosses curveballs their path, they quit and stop chasing their dreams. Why is that? Did they not desire their dreams eagerly enough? Do they truly enjoy their lives as they currently are? Perhaps, perhaps not.

The key, in fact, lies in individuals' attitudes. Not everybody's cut out to hustle and take genuine charge of their lives. When you hustle, you're grabbing control of your life, and you're leaving your comfort zone.

The thing is, some individuals are satisfied with whatever they have going for them right now. They do not have that ambition, that burning enthusiasm to see their dreams reawaken. Which's fine, that's their right, their decision.

Maybe they have actually ended up being cynical and jaded. They have actually seen far a lot of individuals fall short, and just an extremely little minority be successful, so they believe they simply do not have what it requires to beat the odds. In their heads, they have actually already fallen short.

However, you do not need to follow in their footprints. You do not have to feel the same way. You do not have to feel dissuaded each time you find out about somebody who's fallen short at their side hustles.

You Manage Your Mind

The human mind is remarkable. It may either press you to pursue your dreams regardless of what it requires or TO bury it long prior to you even doING a thing about it. However, your thoughts and your mind aren't independent of who you are as an individual. The reality is, YOU manage your mind.

With that stated, if you wish to alter your life, then you have to leave your comfort zone. You are never going to see success if you carry on doing the identical things repeatedly again.

When you go into the realm of side entrepreneurship and hustling, you have to alter how you think. If you have actually got an unfavorable frame of mind, then you definitely need to alter it to a favorable one.

If you do not, then you will never ever get anyplace, you are going to be stuck doing the identical tasks up until you pass away. The identical tasks that provide you with mediocre, unpleasant, and eventually, dissatisfied life.

Have a "Why"

If you wish to be successful in your side hustle, then you have to, firstly, comprehend your "why." Why do you wish to be successful? What do you wish to attain with your side hustle? More cash? Liberty from the rat race?

No matter what the reason, you have to constantly remember your "why" due to the fact that it will be an uphill struggle. There are going to be times when you are going to feel so worn out, when you are going to feel like the planet is conspiring versus you to fall short. You are going to think that your side hustle is not bringing you any nearer to your objectives. When that time arrives,think about your "why," and you are going to feel your inspiration returning.

Have the Appropriate Goals

Your attitude plays a vital part in your side hustle success. If you do not desire your dreams enough, then maybe you're pursuing the incorrect objectives?

You have to get your attitude appropriate prior to trying to do a thing. If you do not, you will be suffering for months and years, questioning why you can't summon the inspiration to do what has to be done. You are going to just be postponing your success, and each step of the path, you are going to feel like you are drowning!

Nevertheless, if you're pursuing objectives that you're enthusiastic about and you have actually got the appropriate attitude for, then you can anticipate different outcomes. This effective mix is what differentiates effective business owners and side hustlers from wannabes and failures.

So, put in the time to learn more about yourself, prepare your attitude, and ask yourself if you're prepared to handle one of the greatest obstacles in your life.

Chapter 2: Know What Your Unique Talents And Abilities Are

You've most likely got a great deal of talents and abilities that you are able to put to great use. However, given that you've got a finite amount of spare time (if you work full-time at your job), then you have to select a lucrative side hustle that is going to assist to optimize your time.

For starters, you could take stock of your distinct talents and capabilities. You can begin by jotting down your work experiences, and after that, note down the skillsets you utilized to do those jobs. If you got any random abilities in the process, note them down too.

This procedure is necessary so you can determine which chances will be great for you. You can then additionally examine the need and marketability of your capabilities due to the fact that, as you most likely recognize, not all abilities are made equal.

Low-Value vs. High-Value Skills

Low-value and general skills most likely won't get you an additional thousand dollars immediately. You are going to have lots of competitors because there is a fairly lower barrier to entry, suggesting a great deal of individuals may do these simple side jobs.

However, if you select a side hustle that necessitates higher-value and more technical capabilities, then odds are, you are going to have less competitors. Based upon the need for those capabilities, you are going to have the ability to generate more additional money monthly than with a low-skill side hustle.

For example, let's suppose you're quite experienced at babysitting, creating sites and copywriting. Which of these do you believe is going to be most lucrative?

With babysitting, you do not actually require distinct capabilities. If you like babies and you know your way with them, then you may quickly end up being a sitter. With this reasoning, anybody trying to find a sitter can, in theory, discover one rapidly, provided, obviously, they pay competitive rates.

When it concerns website design and writing, not everybody has these capabilities. This suggests that the pool of excellent web designers or copywriters will be a lot tinier than the pool of feasible sitters. The thing is, great web designers and copywriters are quite sought after, and that is why they are able to command higher-than-average costs for their services.

Going by the instance above, which side hustle will you select? Do you wish to end up being a sitter, a web designer or a copywriter? I wager the majority of you are going to pick either a web design or copywriting side hustle. Besides, if you have actually just got 20 free hours weekly to deal with your side hustle, then you wish to maximize it. Why deal with a low-priced hustle (for example, $15/hour) when you can deal with something which pays $30-$ 100 an hour? Consider just how much additional money you are going to be bringing in for the identical quantity of time!

Cash VS Fulfillment

If you want to ultimately leave your day job, then having a good-paying side hustle is a necessity. This is why you need to understand your strengths and your capabilities, so you may put them to excellent use and earn some nice money at the same time!

You believe you're a quite capable author and/or web designer, however, you do not wish to invest all your leisure time becoming stressed about work with clients. You currently have enough of that at your job, so you simply wish to do a side hustle where you can relax. Well, that's your call.

To be sincere, there's no right or incorrect way here. All of us have various objectives. For a few of you, you desire a side hustle which may supply you with additional money. For others, you desire something that is going to ultimately substitute your day job. And for some, you wish to do something you actually delight in and still make a couple of dollars out of it.

If you discover babysitting more satisfying as a side hustle than website design or copywriting, then that's completely fine. If that's your enthusiasm, then follow what your heart claims. There's no point working on a side hustle you will dislike or despise ultimately!

It's much better to do what you truly wish to do. When you're enthusiastic about something, it's simpler for you to discover methods to make it grow. You could possibly turn your childcare side hustle into something larger!

For example, you can most likely utilize babysitting as a foot in the door to larger possibilities in the future. You may use your website design and writing services to the kids' moms and dads. So, you are going to basically be striking 2 birds with a single stone!

Ultimately, the success of your side hustle is going to depend upon your dedication. You are going to discover it tough to devote to something you do not delight in, regardless of how competent or gifted you might be.

If you trust in what you're doing and you're delighted doing it, then great for you. Stick to a side hustle which feels appropriate for you. Listen to your heart. Or else, you will regret it in the future.

Chapter 3: Capitalize On Your Strengths and Outsource Everything Else

Do you trust the phrase "time is money?" In case you do, then you understand that your time is far better devoted doing things you're proficient at. You may then leave the remainder (the stuff you're average or terrible at) to individuals who are way more effective than you.

In the start, it might be completely fine to do all the things in your side hustle business all on your own. Nevertheless, as soon as your business begins growing, then you have to think about contracting out those activities that slow you down or those that you do not especially delight in.

This is particularly beneficial if you still have a day job-- you may just do so much! If you insist on doing all the things yourself, then you will just grow slower.

Use Your Time Wisely

If you have actually got the cash even prior to getting going with your side hustle, then immediately, it is going to be simpler for you to scale your business from the beginning! This indicates you can purchase the resources and tools you require to be successful.

You can merely concentrate on doing what you know best and contract out the remainder. You do not have to go through the procedure of dealing with your side business all by your lonely self.

Sadly, nevertheless, not too many individuals will be this fortunate. If you are like most individuals who do not have substantial trust funds or a healthy savings account, then do not stress.

You can still be successful at your side hustle, it will simply require a bit longer since you will do all the things from scratch. Do not contrast your development to others. You will simply wind up pitying yourself, and your self-confidence and your inspiration are going to most likely take a nosedive.

Let me offer you an instance. If you pick blogging, then you might have to do all the things yourself in the beginning. You are going to compose all the material, construct your website, promote your stuff on numerous social networking channels, and so on.

Doing all these things is going to cost you lots of hours, possibly hundreds! However, you'd want to do it anyhow since you're enthusiastic about blogging. You do not mind doing all the dirty work. As a matter of fact, you treasure the learning experience.

When you lastly prosper, you are going to get hundreds or countless individuals reading your article. In case you monetize your website effectively, then you might make a great quantity of cash from your blog site.

You understand that in case you include more premium material to the website, then there's an excellent likelihood your profits will increase. So, now you have to decide. Do you contract out the production of the content or do you do keep on doing all the things yourself?

In case you choose to contract out, you are going to post more posts on your website than in case you continue doing it alone. You are going to have the ability to grow your social presence much quicker. With outsourcing, you're basically duplicating yourself, so you get more work performed in less time!

Should You Outsource?

Outsourcing requires cash. However, do not see it in a negative way. Rather, see it as an investment in your business. You have to invest cash so you can generate income.

Now, working with the appropriate people to assist you with your business isn't precisely simple. In case you head to a website such as Upwork, you are going to most likely get lots of candidates. You'd have to shortlist the ones you believe will be a great fit, and after that, you need to devote a bit of time towards interviewing them.

Doing all these will require some time. And by the end of everything, the freelancer you employed might wind up being just great on paper, however, will not be a great match for your requirements. So, you have to do all the things all over once again.

Outsourcing includes its own share of headache-inducing issues. When you discover a great contractor, you are going to have to train them up on your procedures and systems. They most likely won't get the hang of it immediately. That suggests a couple of weeks until you're lastly pleased, and you feel sufficiently comfy to provide some freedom on how to do their tasks.

Whether you're working with employees or freelancers, remember that it is essential to develop healthy relationships with everybody. In case you appreciate individuals working for you, then they are going to appreciate you as well. They are going to be more dedicated to assisting you to grow your enterprise.

Chapter 4: Have a Plan

Preparation is crucial. Without an excellent strategy, you might just as well be playing in the dark. You're nearly certain to fall short. If you wish to boost your odds of success (and who would not?), then it's a necessity that you plan out your side hustle idea and have a sound plan.

You understand your strengths and your weak points much better than anybody. If you claim you're bad at preparation, then you better figure out a method to move 'preparation' to your strengths column. If you believe that you can't do it all alone, then do not hesitate to request assistance from friends and family.

Ask for help with your side hustle plan. As the phrase goes, several heads are more effective than one. Do a brain dump and jot down all the things you can consider, even those you believe are unreasonable. You are going to have the chance to modify your ideas in the future.

Lists vs. Mind Maps

To arrange your strategies, you may utilize either a straightforward linear list or you could utilize a mind map.

With linear lists, it may be difficult to realize if you have actually got a really, lengthy list. You'd have to scroll down, and it may be frustrating and disorienting simultaneously. If you have actually got strategies that resemble one another, it's tough to demonstrate that on a linear list.

Mind maps, however, offer a more sensible and more orderly method to see your ideas. Its non-linear and free format permits you to quickly move plans around, link comparable strategies and group them together. It's likewise a lot simpler to get a bird's eye view of your approach on a mind map.

To summarize, mind maps are superior tools for the preparation procedure than a linear list. There's are a lot of mind-mapping software applications. You may check out an app such as Mindomo or Bubble. Their free-forever variations enable you to produce approximately 3 mind maps.

Your Advantage

One extremely crucial thing you have to think about when you plan out your side hustle approach is your competitive advantage.

What is your distinct selling proposal? What do you have that your rivals do not? Why should anybody work with you rather than your competitors?

Learn the responses to these, and you may utilize that as your selling point when you head out into the world and begin reaching out to possible customers. They will ask those difficult questions, so you have to prepare your responses in advance. And it's very crucial to trust in those responses!

You can't simply state you're better than the competitors since that's what your partner and your parents informed you. No, you have to do more than that. Be creative if you have to, however, you have to offer a sure-fire and strong reason why individuals ought to offer you the time of day.

Branding

Another thing you ought to think about is your branding. Now, you might believe this isn't all that essential. You might believe you're simply beginning a "little" side hustle, and you do not have to consider this branding aspect.

If you wish to see your side hustle prosper and you desire individuals coming to you rather than you heading to them, then you have to find out how to brand yourself as somebody your target market will wish to work with.

If you do the branding properly, then your marketing efforts are going to be a lot simpler. Individuals are going to start to know and believe your brand. In the total scheme of things, branding simply might be the secret component to your side hustle's success!

It's in The Details

There's a prominent phrase that says, the devil is in the details. At this moment, you might believe you can rush through the details and simply figure things out. Nevertheless, if you choose to follow this path, then you might remain in for some nasty "surprises" along the road. Surprises that you might have been stayed clear of if you have actually just made an effort to plan things out.

You wish to decrease difficulties and barriers. You wish to be ready when they do occur, that's why you plan things ahead of time. If you do not, you will simply wind up hindering your course to success. You're reading this guide due to the fact that you wish to be successful, not fall short.

It's all rather easy truly-- you may either be reactive or proactive. As you most likely realize, prevention is more desirable than remedy. So, it's far better to be proactive and to get ready for whatever might happen than to be reactive when things take place.

Chapter 5: Examine And Confirm Your Idea

Escaping the coziness of your job is a frightening idea, particularly if you have actually never ever once tried to do something so extreme prior. Or, maybe you have, however, you fell short.

Well, there's a method to decrease failure, which is by evaluating and confirming your side hustle idea. This strategy is going to assist you in writing off the side hustles that will not be worth investing your time in just since they will not pay.

Based upon the side hustle you select, you might have to invest some cash in verifying your concept and seeing if it is going to do well or not. This implies you might have to purchase (or borrow or lease) certain resources and tools so you may do your testing.

Maintain your costs to a minimum for now. You do not wish to go all-in and invest countless dollars in tools which you will not have any usage for in the future!

Examine Your Competition

What is your competition doing? What are their items? Their marketing approaches? Why are individuals purchasing their items or utilizing their services? What could you do more effectively? Could you beat them, particularly if they've been around for quite a while?

Ask yourself this, if you were a consumer, would you purchase your items? Or would you visit the competitors and purchase from them? Why or why not? Based upon your response, you ought to have a decent clue on where you stand.

If your rivals are active on social networks, do not hesitate to follow them. It's not unlawful.

Besides, they're practically publishing publically. Research which kinds of content get the best engagement from their fans. Then produce a list of what you have to do so you may do much better.

At this moment, you might feel like David taking on Goliath. Do not fret, simply take it all in stride. You are performing this analysis due to the fact that you do not wish to squander your time contending versus other businesses when you never ever had a shot. You're doing this due to the fact that you wish to boost your chances of success. You do not wish to devote months and years working on a side hustle just to learn that you simply do not have what it requires to prosper!

Acquire Feedback

You ought to plainly determine who your customers or target market are. You wish to optimize your efforts. You don't want to squander your money and time attempting to place your deal ahead of individuals who just aren't interested. Rather, you wish to get your deal ahead of the appropriate people, those who are going to, in fact, invest and work with you!

So, to make certain your target market will like what you bring to the table, then you have to acquire feedback from individuals who match your target demographics.

Suppose, for example, your target customers are small companies in California with 1-2 workers. You may attempt searching for individuals in your personal network who fit that profile. You may likewise publish your question on social networks and/or pertinent online forums.

Present your offer and inquire if it's a thing they would have an interest in. If yes, why? If no, why? Obtaining in-depth responses will assist you in enhancing your offer and boost your possibilities of success.

Do not forget to thank individuals for their time. You're attempting to develop a brand name, and you ought to constantly try to find chances to place your brand name on top of individuals' minds.

Have a 'Soft' Launch

You do not wish to go all out at this moment, considering that you're still in the procedure of verifying your idea. So, if you're offering a physical item in your shop, then you might not wish to have hundreds of products. What will occur to those if your target market does not bite? That is going to actually equate to cash down the drain if you do not get to offer your stock.

This is specifically accurate if you're doing eCommerce as a side hustle. You wish to make certain there's a sustainable and genuine need for your item. Otherwise, you might be squandering your energy on something which will never ever work.

Now, if your launch ends up being effective, then you have actually most likely got a successful side hustle on your hands. Nevertheless, if not, then do not hesitate to return to the drawing board. Do not consider it a failure-- you're doing these tests to discover the ideal and most lucrative side hustle!

Chapter 6: Have A Strong Marketing Plan

If you're nervous and shy and you're frightened at the idea of speaking with random businesses and individuals, then you're in for a surprise. Your side hustle will never ever blast off if you do not head out there and let individuals realize you're open for business.

So, prior to you even consider which marketing method to utilize, you have to determine how you may toughen up as soon as possible. You have to have self-confidence so you may sell and promote yourself to possible customers.

Place yourself in the shoes of your potential customers: would you wish to work with somebody who exhibits self-confidence or somebody who does not? I am certain you are going to select the former.

As soon as you have actually developed your self-confidence in your capabilities and believe you are able to provide what your side hustle is about, then it's time to promote yourself to your target market.

Now, the twist is that there are various kinds of marketing strategies you are able to utilize. Look around you, how are your rivals marketing their brand? Is it working? Should you do the identical or should you search for another method, so you can take advantage of another, less saturated market?

What you eventually choose is going to depend upon your market. However, for starters, let me offer you a concept of the most typical marketing methods which are able to work for lots of side hustles:

Word of Mouth

Word of mouth is most likely the easiest kind of marketing there is, yet it's likewise among the most successful. How many times have you purchased an item or registered for a service your friends and family have suggested? Or, how frequently do you ask them for suggestions?

The reason that word of mouth works so effectively is that we have a tendency to rely on the judgment of individuals we personally know. So, when they state you ought to take a look at this brand-new place on 9th Street, then you are going to go check it out as quickly as you get some spare time.

For your side hustle, it is necessary that you utilize your existing network of buddies. Ask to assist you in getting the word out about your product. If anybody inquires why they ought to work with you, they are able to quickly attest your capabilities, your integrity or talent.

When you begin obtaining some customers, ensure you go above and beyond. Provide a great deal of worth and ensure they have a really favorable experience. If you do this, you will not even have to ask your customers to assist in getting the word out about you, they are going to be pleased to do it!

Door to Door

This type of marketing approach is going to just work effectively for side hustles which pinpoint the local population. If you have actually got side hustle on the internet, then this might not be the appropriate marketing approach for you.

For this marketing approach to be successful, you have to make an individual connection with individuals you will be speaking with. You're going to be knocking on their doors and speaking to them personally, so speak with them like individuals. Do not be aggressive and pushy since you will simply get the door knocked in your face, or even worse, have security actually called on you!

For door-to-door marketing to be successful, you have to be creative. Do not simply knock on individuals' doors, provide your card, and leave suddenly. Rather, what you ought to do is present yourself and let them know you have actually begun a brand-new business. State something such as, "If you require my aid, here's my card. Please do not be reluctant to reach out."

For example, in case your side hustle is painting individuals' walls, then you might wish to state something along the lines of "When your paint begins to fade, simply offer me a call, and I am going to be happy to provide my initial price even if you call me a couple of years in the future."

See, you're not pressing them to utilize your service immediately. You're simply sharing what it is you do and how you can assist them, which is all there is to it, actually.

Social Media

Everybody's on social networks these days. Whether you have actually got an offline or online side hustle, you can gain from the power of social network marketing.

Initially, you have to understand where your target customers are hanging out. Are they on LinkedIn, Facebook, Twitter, Instagram, or some other social network?

Then develop a good profile and make certain it matches your branding. Post content which demonstrates your competence. Do not publish anything ridiculous which is going to make you appear completely unprofessional.

Start connecting to your target customers. Follow them and/or leave considerate comments on their posts. You can likewise send them private messages, however, do not be pushy and aggressive. You wish to acquire their trust, so they are going to work with you, you do not wish to startle them. In case you send them a personal message, ensure it will be worth their while.

Social network marketing has the capability to expand your side hustle greatly. However, be really mindful of how you set about doing it. If you frustrate a lot of individuals, you can rapidly lose your credibility, and you might have to begin once again from scratch!

Chapter 7: Have Realistic Timelines And Goals

At this moment, your side hustle is precisely what it states, you deal with it on the side, indicating it's not your full-time thing. You're generally working on your hustle on days when you do not have routine work and even before/after you head to work. Clearly, your schedule is going to depend upon you and how occupied you are at the workplace.

When you're simply beginning with your side hustle, you have to be reasonable with your objectives. Sure, you might believe your hustle's got actual potential, and you believe you may make it grow to make 10x your wage or something similar.

However, actually, do you believe that you have that much time to commit to your business?

Consider it completely, otherwise, you'd wind up frustrating yourself majorly.

Setting Goals

You can go for lofty and enthusiastic goals. You can likewise go for exceptionally simple objectives. Or you can go for the middle-of-the-road one, not too effortless, not too tough, just right.

When you go for enthusiastic ones, you might wind up worrying yourself to death. You are going to undertake more work than you can deal with, you are going to begin missing out on due dates, you are going to have customers suffering poor quality work, and so on. You do not desire that. When you press yourself to accomplish something you merely can not physically do, then you're actually destroying yourself.

On the other end, if you go for objectives which are way too simple for you, then you might wind up procrastinating. You are going to think, "I could do that job in a day. I am going to do it tomorrow. I am going to simply go play on my computer today." So, you wind up refraining from doing anything and squander a great deal of time.

The appropriate objectives would be something that is going to challenge you or press you to utilize your time sensibly. You will not put things off, and simultaneously, you won't drive yourself up the wall. In this manner, you're extremely effective, and you eventually bring yourself nearer to your objectives.

Your Timelines

There are 3 various goal timelines. When it pertains to your side hustles, you may establish short-term, long-term and life goals.

For short-term ones, think about what you wish to attain with your side hustle over the following couple of weeks or months. Ask yourself just how much you wish to make in the next month approximately, and how you intend to accomplish that objective. Having a daily, weekly and regular monthly to-do list would be also advantageous. It is going to assist in maintaining you on track and making certain you adhere to what you have actually intended.

For your long-term objectives, think about where you desire your side hustle to be in a couple of years. Do you believe you are still going to be working on your own? Or do you believe your small business is going to have grown already and you have a team to assist you? Or do you believe you are going to still be employed at your job?

For your life objectives, this is what you want the most. What do you wish to attain with your side hustle? Where do you ultimately see yourself numerous years from now? You'd most likely be the CEO of your own business, the one that began with your side hustle. Or perhaps your objective is to see your neighborhood enterprise end up being an international one. Whatever your life objective might be, ensure your long-term and short-term objectives line up with it.

Continuously Reassess your Goals

Your objectives aren't carved in stone. In time, you might recognize that a few of your objectives might not be possible. So, you have to calibrate and adjust as needed.

There's no requirement to worry if you do not accomplish your objectives as intended. Merely reassess your objectives and attempt to come up with something more attainable.

For instance, if you discover that your aim was too challenging or too convoluted to attain within the timeframe you picked, then maybe you might wish to change the timeframe or scrap that objective entirely.

Nobody will tell you off. If you have to alter your objectives, then so be it. You're most likely simply a one-man show at this moment in your side hustle journey. There's no requirement to be so tough on yourself.

Taking pleasure in the journey and the process is essential. You have a huge objective you wish to attain at some point. You won't have the ability to do that if you slam yourself each time you make an incorrect move. Learn from your failures and errors. It's the only manner in which you will grow as a business owner, as a hustler, and as an individual.

Chapter 8: Your Side Hustle Needs to Be Separate From Your Job

If you value your job, then you would not wish to lose it, specifically not when your side hustle has actually hardly even begun. Even when your side hustle gets to the point where you're bringing in more cash than at your job, you might still wish to maintain your job.

If you work at a job you truly like and take pleasure in and you discover it extremely satisfying, then, of course, remain in it. If this is you, then great for you. Not everybody is as fortunate as you. So, here are some suggestions to assist in maintaining your side hustle different from your day job:

Do Not Cheat at Your Job

Among the greatest no-no's of owning a side hustle is working on it while you're on paid time. Even if you have actually got the dullest job on the planet, if your time is compensated by somebody else, then you should not be disrespecting them by focusing on your side hustle covertly. If you get seen, you might lose your job.

Also, if your side hustle is likewise rather linked to the things you do at work, then you ought to make sure not to get lured into providing your services to your work clients. That's referred to as poaching. Your company may sue you for breach of contract, which's a thing you ought to wish to stay clear of at all expense.

You have to appreciate boundaries in between your hustle and work. If you're employed, then you have to play by your company's guidelines.

Time Management

Time management is really essential when it concerns side hustling. Given that you have actually just got a minimal quantity of time every day, and you have to split that with work and other individual dedications, then ensure that each and every single moment you allocate to your side hustle is, in fact, devoted to working on it!

However, doing this could be extremely hard, specifically in case your side hustle is at home. There are simply far too many interruptions-- you have actually got Netflix, animals, children, and so on. It's so difficult to refuse buddies inviting you to head for a night out throughout weekends. However, you have to develop the guts to state "no." You might seem like a party-pooper, however truly, it's all for the best.

You need to lessen random 'play' times as that can seriously interrupt your concentration and is going to actually destroy your plans. Make your to-do list and your schedule ahead of time and ensure you stay with it.

Having a regimen is crucial to side hustle success. If you have random things interrupting your schedule constantly, you are going to discover it difficult to discover a rhythm so you may work in peace.

For side hustles which need focus and creativity, you typically have to enter a 'zone' prior to doing anything. If you allow yourself to be sidetracked by the smallest things, then you won't truly achieve a lot.

Have Boundaries

You have to set physical limits once you focus on your side hustle. For example, if you develop designs or write, you most likely need to have some solitude so you may get your creative juices going.

If you do not live by yourself, then you have to discover some area all to yourself. If you have actually got an extra bedroom (or any other space for that matter), then utilize that as your workplace.

Inform individuals you reside with that when you're in your particular area, you don't want to be interrupted unless there's an emergency situation. You can set up a sign which states something to that effect to hinder anybody from accidentally troubling you.

When it pertains to customers, you likewise have to establish boundaries. Based upon your side hustle, it may be crucial to point out that you do have a full-time job, so they do not call you whenever they want.

Some customers might stress when they do not speak with you quickly, so they call you. It's much better to be straight up about your routine than have them believe you're at their beck and call.

If they actually, truly require something done quickly, like it's an issue of life or death, then you might have to make an exception (simply ensure it's really an emergency situation). You may maybe take an early lunch break at work to go do the immediate activity from your side hustle customer.

Simply keep in mind not to be a doormat due to the fact that it may be actually simple for individuals to take you for granted. Stand your ground and follow the guidelines you have actually established. Your boundaries may actually spare you peace of mind!

Chapter 9: Have A Routine

How many spare hours do you have on a workday? How many spare hours do you have on your rest days? How many hours do you require for your individual regimens? For sleep?

There are a lot of reasons why you have to produce and adhere to a rigorous side hustle routine. For one, you just have 24 hours a day. That's set, non-negotiable., you have actually have to squeeze in your day job, your side hustle, and all the things else inside this timeframe.

If you do not wish to perish young, then you have to make certain not to stress yourself. You have to spend time looking after your body. You have to evaluate your physical, emotional and mental health every now and then. The explanation for this is due to the fact that if you get ill, then you do not arrive to work; it's as easy as that.

Plan Your Day Out

Preparing your schedule each and every day is going to assist in guaranteeing that you stay clear of handling more than you can reasonably manage. You can just do so much in a day.

For instance, if you have actually got a blog site as a side hustle, then plan the number of words you need to be composing every day. If that does not work for you, then think of the number of posts you can reasonably create and publish in a week.

Keep in mind that consistency is crucial to success in nearly everything, and it's particularly crucial for side hustles! Due to the fact that you're your own boss, you have to construct your day so you do not set about procrastinating and doing things you actually should not be doing!

Optimize Your Time

Strictly adhering to your schedule is going to assist in optimizing your time. Determine a method to do activities that are going to assist in optimizing your time. Have a system in position or a procedure that is going to assist you from getting a customer to sending their deliverables in the most effective manner.

You might begin with a model of your system (let's refer to it as system A), however, someplace along the road, you are going to discover it's not as efficient as system B. If this occurs, then you have to change. You have to do whatever it requires as effectively as feasible.

You can't simply state you are going to stick to system A since that's what you thought of initially, or that's what's located on your whiteboard or wherever. Do not hesitate to alter strategies; you have to do what it requires to optimize your time!

Do One Thing at a Time

Multitasking is an important capability, however, oftentimes, it may slow you down. It's so simple to lose focus when you multitask. It's simple to get overwhelmed by the various things you have to do.

For instance, in case you're doing a bit of client work, viewing television and taking a look at social networks simultaneously, you most likely will not get a lot work done. When it's time to focus on your side hustle, switch off the diversions.

Place your phone on quiet mode if it won't be utilized in your side work. Switch off the television. Take the needed actions to make certain you provide your complete attention to what you're dealing with.

Believe me, you will get numerous things done when you have actually gotten rid of the interruptions. You may even have the ability to complete your activities in advance of your schedule. When you do this, then you may award yourself by enjoying some television up until it's time for you to deal with the following activity on your to-do list.

Treat Yourself

It's an exceptionally gratifying sensation when you cross off things on your to-do list. When you're on a routine, it's often tough to consider treating yourself when your planned downtime is 5 days away. Now, the important thing is, you do not have to spend lavishly, however, do not shy away from treating yourself either.

For example, if you managed to do all the things on your to-do list for the day, then you may treat yourself with an additional hour. Or maybe you have your preferred Chinese food delivered so you can make the time before the TV a lot more pleasurable. If you complete your to-do list for the week, then treat yourself to a cinema ticket.

Rigorously following a routine-- and for a side hustle at that-- needs discipline and dedication. If you are successful, then you definitely should have whichever reward you have actually got prepared!

Chapter 10: Zero in On What Creates Income

As much as feasible, you wish to create some profits each time you focus on your side hustle. So, you have actually got to find out how you can simplify your systems and your procedures to come up with the most successful 'formula.'

As you currently understand, not all side hustles are made alike. Certain side hustles are simple, while some are a tad more complex and need extensive preparation. If you've taken part in an 'easier' side hustle, then creating income is as easy as providing your service to your next-door neighbors.

Now, when it pertains to producing income for more complicated side hustles, then you would wish to concentrate your time on activities, which, in fact, are going to bring in the cash. Here are some suggestions:

Concentrate on Your Target Market

Prior to beginning your side hustle, you ought to currently have at least a concept of who your perfect customers and clients are. Suppose, for example, that you wish to tutor children. Prior to you walking around promoting your business, you ought to currently understand what sort of topics you will tutor on, what grade levels you will deal with, and so on

If you're babysitting, then you might wish to just look after kids at particular ages. If you're not comfy being left alone with a young child or a baby, then that's great. You can simply pick to babysit kids 4 years of age and over.

In a lot of cases, developing a purchaser persona of your target market is valuable. It's simpler for you to develop offers which they are going to discover fascinating.

For example, if you have a dropshipping business on the side, you'd most likely be marketing your business on different social network channels (you have to invest both money and time). If you're pursuing the incorrect individuals, then you won't get a lot of sales. Nevertheless, if you concentrate your attention (and your advertisements) on individuals who are going to really gain from purchasing your items, then you might make a great deal of cash!

So, that's what you are after. You wish to optimize your ROI. And the ideal method to do that is by placing your brand name and your deal ahead of the appropriate audience. If you do not, then your cash will actually go down the drain.

Bring in and Support Leads

The significance of lead generation can't ever be downplayed. Without a pipeline filled with leads, you are going to be having a hard time surviving.

Without excellent leads, how will you produce income?

A sound marketing method is going to assist you in filling your pipeline with quality leads. However, you can't simply leave it at that. Rather, you need to support your leads, so they ultimately end up being paying customers.

With lead generation, you may either do it by hand or you may automate the whole procedure. For manual lead generation, you may request recommendations from your existing network, like your buddies and even customers. You can attempt providing discount rates to anybody who sends some brand-new consumers your path.

For automated lead gen, this is primarily utilized by online businesses. You may establish a landing page with a really alluring deal. When individuals download or have a look at your deal, they enter their contact information on the page. All you need to do then is to call them, and after that, do your finest to transform them into paying customers.

Customer Service is The Key

Some individuals undervalue customer support. They believe there's no cash to be had in supplying great customer support. However, obviously, this is not just correct, however, it can wipe out your side hustle totally!

Dissatisfied customers can quickly go on the internet and post about their disappointment with your business. Word can rapidly spread out about you. Individuals who have not heard of you are going to search for you. When they read the poor reviews, they will go somewhere else. They won't risk their cash with you.

Nevertheless, if you treat your clients properly, if you provide your guarantee, then they are going to be delighted. They are going to be loyal, they are going to be repeat clients, and most importantly, they are going to tell their buddies everything about you. As you understand, word of mouth is among the most helpful types of marketing. Pretty quickly, you are going to have more leads than you can handle!

Chapter 11: How To Avoid Burning Out

Working full-time could be difficult. Dealing with a side hustle can take your tension levels to a whole new level. Regardless of how enthusiastic you are about your side hustle, even if it's your most cherished thing to do on the planet, there is going to come a time when you are going to begin feeling stressed out. So, how can you stay clear of the side hustle burnout? Here are a couple of suggestions:

Delegate or Contract Out

You do not need to be a one-person company permanently. Certainly, being hands-on with your business is fantastic, however, you have actually just got a single body. And that body still has a full-time job to address.

When you begin feeling the heat, and you believe that the walls are enclosing around you, then maybe it's about time you hand over or contract out a few of the lesser activities.

Obviously, discovering somebody to assist you is going to indicate investing both money and time. You are going to invest time educating them and getting them competent, and you are going to be compensating them for their time.

The concern would be, should you offer all your secrets? Do you tell them all the things about your business enterprise, the details? You most likely can if you believe your contractor or worker sufficiently, but for one of the most part, it's most likely ideal not to.

Stop the Comparison Game

Regardless of how tough you attempt, another person is going to constantly be more effective, more attractive, more popular, more skilled, and so on than you. If you're utilizing your side hustle as a way to take on somebody else, then you will never ever win.

For example, let's suppose you have a youth buddy who, in some way, succeeded to rise through the ranks and now owns a million-dollar house and drives great automobiles. You wish to succeed as your buddy.

So, you begin a side hustle where you intend to ultimately end up being a millionaire. You do whatever you can to prosper. However, 5 years later on, you're no closer to your buddy's socioeconomic class. Possibly you now drive a great automobile, however, you still reside in an identical home. You have actually done all the things and you're still a couple of million dollars poorer than your buddy. You end up being disillusioned, you end up being depressed, and ultimately, you quit.

Rather than being jealous of your buddy's success, how about you concentrate on how far you've come? For instance, let's suppose that in the 5 years you have actually worked on your side hustle, your earnings have more than doubled or tripled, your lifestyle has actually enhanced, and you're now in a place to quit your day job permanently.

This is why you have to be conscious and grateful for what you do have. Contrasting yourself to others is one fast method to burn yourself out, so do not do it. Find out how to value your achievements and yourself, regardless of how little they might appear to you today.

Have Deadlines

Among the fastest paths to burnout is to set silly due dates on your own. With your side hustle, you're your own boss. You have to strive, however, you likewise have to work intelligently if you desire your side hustle to last more than a week.

Do not take more work than you can manage to deal with. Otherwise, you are going to be required to say "yes" to due dates that will actually drive you insane. You might require the cash, however, it does not suggest that you will destroy yourself for it.

If you have actually got a number of customers providing you a great deal of cash for doing some immediate work over the weekend, then you might have to decline either one of them, or maybe even both of them!

You can attempt to work out the due date, and perhaps one of them is going to accept to move their due date to a later date. Nevertheless, if you actually have to, then do not hesitate to simply decline.

Know How to Take a Break

Can you envision how exhausted you would feel if you worked for 12 months directly without taking one day of rest? Sure, you might receive a day or couple days of rest at your job, however, technically, you're still dealing with your side hustle. So, you're not actually "off," you're simply doing another thing.

When you're simply beginning your side hustle, there might be stretches where you are going to work for weeks without relaxing. However, once you have the ability to, once you complete your initial task, you ought to treat yourself by taking a time-out.

You do not have to purchase an airplane ticket to some exotic area abroad (though you might if you actually wish to). You can simply chill at your home for a whole day without looking at your e-mails or pondering on your side hustle or day job. Simply delight in your "me time."

Whenever you get to a significant turning point, treat yourself to something great. Obtain a body massage or purchase yourself that coat or bag you have actually been considering purchasing for months now!

If you end up being stuck doing identical things repeatedly once again, you will get bored ultimately. If you wish to discover how you can restore your enjoyment for both your side hustle and your job, then you have to do something distinct.

You can't most likely do much about your job, however, when it comes to your side hustle, possibly rather than developing some graphics today, you might wish to do a different side job rather.

How about attempting babysitting or dog walking? Or perhaps go drive an Uber for a couple of hours? Do a thing you do not generally do, a thing which is going to bring you loads of enjoyment!

You do not even have to change up your side hustle. You may go hiking in the mountains or go clubbing during the night or drive to the beach. This simply might offer you the increase you require to rev up your inspiration at your side hustle and at work!

Chapter 12: When to Leave Your Job Safely

So, your side hustle is lastly beginning to blast off, and your future has actually never ever looked so brilliant. You're thrilled at the possibility of working full-time on what was recently your small side project. You most likely feel how Steve Jobs and Bill Gates had when they were lastly prepared to vacate their garages to introduce their dazzling items to the world!

However, how do you understand when it's risk-free to leave your job? Do you simply make that choice when you feel like it? Well, the reality is, you can leave anytime you like. However, do not blame any person else if your side hustle crashes and burns.

So, here are a couple of indications you're prepared to leave your day job and go after your side hustle full-time:

Your Side Hustle is Earning You More Money

This is, in fact, a great tipping point for many side hustlers. The minute their side hustle generates more cash than their job, they simply up and leave. However, is it actually a wise choice?

The response is "yes" and "no." "Yes," if the side earnings are sufficiently steady, that is, your hustle has actually been regularly producing more cash than your primary job for a number of months now. "No," if it's not steady enough, that is, your side earnings ebbs and flows, and there's no warranty that the following months' revenues are going to suffice.

However, exactly what does "way more money" imply precisely? Well, that truly depends upon your living costs and you. Some individuals might be happy with side earnings 2x their wage, while some are going to just accept if it's 5x or

10x their wages. Find out your number and utilize it as a criterion to determine if you're prepared to take the leap.

You Have Enough Savings

Simply in the event your side hustle does not work out, what will you do for cash? How will you have the ability to sustain your way of life if you lose both your side earnings and your wage?

Having an emergency fund is the highest priority. Numerous financial experts suggest having at least 6 months of your regular monthly earnings in a savings account. It needs to be liquid, so when an emergency situation hits, you may quickly get the cash.

You can't invest it into monetary instruments such as stocks where the risk is far too big. Sure, if you're fortunate and you "time" the marketplace wonderfully, you might wind up with a fairly substantial quantity. Nevertheless, the reverse might likewise hold true. You may just as rapidly lose a big quantity of your hard-earned money in the blink of an eye!

So, it's finest to be on the side of caution and simply leave your emergency fund in a high-interest savings account, so inflation does not 'eat' it excessively. If your side hustle does not work out, you are going to have a nest egg while you try to regain control.

You Can Scale

You have actually got the bank account and the data to demonstrate that your side hustle is prepared to move on. You're prepared to take it to a higher level. However, you can't do that if you're still connected to your day job. And you understand that the longer you remain at your job, the longer you're postponing your success. So, you do the only logical thing left to do-- you leave your job.

Obviously, prior to doing that, you ought to evaluate and ensure you're not taking a look at your side hustle through rose-colored glasses. Get another person's viewpoint, somebody who can take a look at things from a neutral angle. Perhaps somebody who's been there in your place, a mentor possibly. They may provide you with some important guidance on whether your business is prepared for the spotlight, and if it's not, what you may do to make it prepared.

You're Dedicated to Seeing Your Side Hustle Succeeding

In some cases, you feel it in your bones that you're doing the appropriate thing. When you're truly enthusiastic about your side hustle, and it's what you have actually constantly wished to do, then leaving your day job is most likely an excellent plan.

Invest a bit of time considering the advantages and disadvantages of leaving your job and concentrating on your side business. If you

Printed in Great Britain
by Amazon

79671198R00047

believe the upsides more than surpass the downsides, then, of course, go all out. There's nobody stopping you from taking the bulls by the horn. Simply ensure you have a backup strategy, a fallback, in the event things do not go as intended.

I hope that you enjoyed reading through this book and that you have found it useful. If you want to share your thoughts on this book, you can do so by leaving a review on the Amazon page. Have a great rest of the day.